Zip Zap Man

He paints some cars red.

He paints some cars green.

He paints some sports cars.

He paints some posh cars.

This is Bill. At night, he checks the numbers.

Then he pops on a film.

4

One night, Number 12
sees a film he likes.

He comes up with a plan.

He gets lots of car parts, then ...

... he turns into ...

In town he spots a robber.

Zip! Zap!

Zip Zap Man locks the car.

Zip Zap Man sets
ott the car alarm.

The cops come and get the robber.

Some kids at the fair are stuck up high.

Help!

But Zip Zap Man is there.

Zip! Zap!

The kids can get down.

Then he turns back into Number 12.

Bill has not seen him go.

The next morning, Number 12 is painting cars again. It is dull.

But what have the men seen?

Wow!

Wow!

No one thinks that Number 12 is Zip Zap Man.

He still paints cars.
It is still dull. But at
night, Number 12
is Zip Zap Man!

Zip! Zap!

That is the best job of all!